Rental Property Management Blueprint.

Creating wealth with rental property investing and discovering overwhelming rental property management strategy.

Richard Turner

TABLE OF CONTENTS

2

INTRODUCTION 3

CHAPTER ONE 7

WHAT IS A RENTAL PROPERTY? 7
SEVEN STEPS YOU'LL NEED TO TAKE TO INVEST IN A RENTAL PROPERTY: 9
CONSIDERATIONS FOR YOUR LEASE 18

CHAPTER TWO 23

COMMON RENTAL PROPERTY MISTAKES BEGINNERS MAKE 23

CHAPTER THREE 25

A LANDLORD'S GUIDE TO LATE PAYMENT FEES 25
WHAT IS A LATE FEE? 25
PAYMENT BEST PRACTICES FOR LATE PAYMENT 27
SIX THINGS A RENTAL PROPERTY OWNER CANNOT DO 29

CHAPTER FOUR 35

WHAT IS PROPERTY MANAGEMENT? 35
HOW TO GET AN EXPERIENCED PROPERTY MANAGER FOR A RENTAL PROPERTY 35
TASKS PERFORMED BY RENTAL PROPERTY MANAGER YOU SHOULD KNOW ABOUT 37

PROPERTY MANAGEMENT TIPS FOR THE FIRST TIME BUYERS   39

HOW TO MANAGE RENTAL PROPERTY THE RIGHT WAY.   40

CHAPTER FIVE   46

HOW RENTAL PROPERTIES MAKE MONEY   46

CHAPTER SIX   54

CONCLUSION   54

INTRODUCTION

As a property owner, one of the primary decisions you are going to make is requiring the services of a rental property company to monitor your investment or to become a homeowner and do everything yourself. Making the property manager decision in your rental property investment requires careful consideration, as each strategy justifies its own considerations.

First things first, you have options. As one of the most significant decisions you can make as a rental property owner, identifying and measuring the pros and cons of each path is critical. Managing a rental on your own can be financially rewarding, but at the same time, it also requires a great deal of time and effort. On the other hand, hiring a rental property management company offers a reduction in day-to-day responsibilities, freeing you up to do whatever you want. However, that freedom comes at a cost and can have a positive long-term impact on your rental property empire.

CHAPTER ONE

What Is A Rental Property?

A rental property is a residential or commercial property that is rented or rented to a tenant for a specified period of time. There are short-term rentals, such as vacation rentals, and long-term rentals, such as those with a one- to three-year lease.

Residential rental properties are one- to four-family dwellings, including:

- Single family homes,
- Duplex,
- Triplex

Types of commercial rental properties include:
- Multi-family (apartment complexes),
- Industrial (such as a warehouse or self-storage),
- Office space,
- Commercial space, and
- Multipurpose.

Residential rental properties tend to be more affordable for beginners because they are less expensive. Less money is required up-front and that often means that financing is easier to obtain.

For these reasons, this comprehensive guide to investing in rental properties focuses on residential rentals.

Most investors buy a rental property with the goal of generating positive cash flow - earning more income each month than they spend on expenses. Not all rentals have a positive cash flow initially, but building one is a common goal of investing in rentals.

Owning a rental property is an active form of real estate investment and requires time, dedication, and involvement. Owning is not for everyone. As you will see, there is enormous work required in analyzing, purchasing, identifying standard rental property.

While there are options to outsource some of these active tasks, it is rarely 100% passive and there are always risks.

Do you think investing in a rental property could be a good idea for you? Read on to find out where to start and how to best prepare for the project at hand.

Six steps you'll need to take to invest in a rental property:

1. Determine where you want to invest

Beginning real estate investors often want to buy rental properties in their backyard. That could mean in the same zip code as your current residence, the same city, or the same state. However, this may not be an option depending on the market you live in, nor is it always the best option.

If you live in a neighborhood where property values are at the higher end of the market, the rent may not support a cash flow positive rental property.

Maybe you live in an expensive market like San Francisco, where the median single-family property was $ 1.6 million in July 2019. You may not have the funds available to buy rental property nearby. If that's the case, look elsewhere for your first investment.

While it may be easier to manage a rental that is only 10 minutes from your home rather than two states away, you can invest in any market. If you're not going to invest in your backyard, take a high-level look at other markets, looking for areas that meet these criteria:

The demand for rental properties is high: The supply of housing and vacancy rates are low. Job growth is stable or growing. Economic expansion, job increase, and population increase are perfect indicators.

There are several free and paid resources to help you conduct market research in various areas of the country, including our own guide to the best places to buy rental properties in 2021. Use them to learn about economic increase, housing demand, unemployment rates, median income, and median house prices in different areas.

2. Make a firm decision on what you want to invest in

While single-family rental properties are an investment avenue, they are not the only option. You can have a duplex, a triplex, or something even larger (if you are interested in commercial rentals). Decide if you would also like to own vacation rentals or long-term rental properties.

Regardless of the type of property you choose, it is essential to know what qualities of that type of property are in demand. This includes the size of the unit or house, the number of bedrooms and bathrooms, or possible amenities like a pool or fireplace.

Find out if there is an over saturation or an insufficient supply of a specific property type. You may find, for example, that one area has too many one-bedroom apartments and few two-bedroom apartments available for rent. You can do this by looking at the current inventory on the market on real estate rental industry sites like Zillow, Hot Pads, or ForRent.com. Making out time to confide in a local agent is another great way to find strategic information on the market.

Make sure you know what you are looking for in a rental property, including:

Square feet,

Number of bedrooms or bathrooms,

Type of construction (for example, wood or concrete),

Type of parking available, and

Property type (for example, single-family residence, condo, townhouse, duplex, triplex, or quad).

It is not uncommon to have different sets of criteria for different neighborhoods.

3. *Find possible rental properties to invest in*

Once you have explored down your market and know your criteria, you can look for properties to invest in. There are different methods to discover investment properties.

Search the MLS or work with a real estate agent

The general method to identify potential investment properties is by exploring the Multiple Listing Service (MLS). Websites like Realtor.com and Zillow allow you to configure search parameters and alert you when a new listing matches those criteria.

You can also contact a real estate investment agent in the area and ask them to set up those same alerts. A quality real estate agent can be an excellent source of connections to banks, lenders, contractors, or vendors that will be helpful when purchasing rental property.

They can also bring you pocket listings, which are listings that have not yet been published in the MLS.

Buying a turnkey rental property

Some companies specialize in selling turnkey rental properties. These rentals require little or no work after purchase; this is a passive investment primarily for cash flow. (Of course, no rent is completely passive - you may need to get involved if things take an unexpected turn.)

In most circumstances, the properties have been renovated, have an existing tenant in place, and have a third-party management company that takes care of the owner's responsibilities.

Work with a wholesaler

A real estate wholesaler discovers off-market investment opportunities at lower-market prices. They negotiate a low purchase price with the seller and assign the contract to an outside buyer at a higher price. The wholesaler makes a profit on the difference between the purchase price and the selling price.

Typically, wholesale properties require a 100% cash payment to close. They often need renovations or upgrades as well, so they may not qualify for financing. There are alternative lenders, such as private and hard money lenders, who can help with closing cash and funds to repair the property. However, these lenders can charge high interest rates and only lend money for a short period of time.

While wholesalers may have quality investment opportunities outside of the market, financial difficulties can make working with them difficult.

- *Direct marketing*

Second way to discover a potential rental property to invest in is by organizing a marketing campaign. You can use targeted online marketing or put up bandit posters. Direct mail marketing is another general option.

In a direct mail campaign, an investor sends a series of letters or postcards to out-of-market sellers. Companies like List Source and Data Tree allow you to create and buy lists of people who meet certain criteria. You can search for homeowners in foreclosure or pre-foreclosure, properties that have recently been through probate, or properties that are owned free and royalty-free (without a mortgage).

You can narrow the list by property features, such as the number of bedrooms and bathrooms, or by county, zip code, or city.

You can run your own mailing campaign by typing or handwriting a series of letters or postcards. You can also require the services of a certified company to do the job for you.

4. Analyze the rental property and calculate the numbers

Finding out the net cash flow of a rental property is critical.

To do this, first determine what you will be able to charge in rental income. renetometer is a free tool that allows you to analyze average and average rental rates based on your property's location, size, and property type. If the property is already occupied by a tenant, ensure that the tenant is making a payment for market rental rates; there might be potential to increase the rent.

Always verify that comparable rentals are in similar condition to your property.

After placing the market rent for the property, verify the average availability rate for your specific market based on the type of property you are buying. Use census data or a real estate data tool to obtain this information.

Next, identify all the costs that may be associated with the property, which may include:

- Taxes,
- Property insurance
- Water and sewage,
- Trash,
- Electric,
- Gas,
- Homeowner's association (HOA) fees,
- Advertising,
- Maintenance (the industry standard is 1% to 3% of the property value),
- Lawn care, and
- Property management (if you use an external administrator).

Sparkrental has a free online rental property ROI calculator that analyzes investment and provides total return on investment using cash-over-cash return and capitalization rate.

Most rental properties use a cash return on cash when determining the return on investment. However, the maximum rate is beneficial when investing in a property that has more than one rental unit.

Keep in mind that there is always the possibility that the property will not produce the initially projected profit or return. You could also have unexpected problems throughout the business. There is no "perfect" return on investment, an ideal capitalization rate, or the best monthly cash flow. It all comes down to your personal investment goals, desired rate of return, and risk threshold.

Analyze each rental property and only move forward with the investment (s) that suit your needs.

5. *Get financing (if necessary)*

If you cannot buy the entire property for cash, you will need financing. Start the formality and underwriting process as soon as possible once you have identified an investment. Not all banks make loans to individuals for investment properties; Identify a lender or bank you can work with before the property is under contract.

Most banks require a 20% down payment, but putting more often means a better interest rate. Interest rates are generally higher on investment property loans and can vary depending on the type of property you are buying.

6. *Choose a tenant*

After closing the property, you must choose a tenant. Assessing tenants can mean the difference between a quality tenant who maintains the property and pays on time, or one who is late each month, stops paying altogether, or destroys the property when leaving.

If you do it yourself, make sure your selection process is consistent for all tenants. Know what evaluation questions you want to ask and understand the Fair Housing rules. While it's up to you to determine your requirements, there are some common standards in the residential rental property industry:

Income that meets or exceeds the amount of the rent (three times the amount of the rent is the gold standard).

Work history consistent with a current and stable job.

If you discover a misdemeanor, criminal record, eviction, or other unfavorable outcome during the screening process, ask questions to learn more. If the potential tenant does not meet your housing requirements (which must be within the Fair Housing guidelines), you do not have to rent to them.

Remember that even the best screening process can result in a tenant breaking the lease.

Considerations for your lease

A lease is the binding agreement between the tenant and the landlord that outlines the responsibilities of each party. This often includes:

- If the tenant can have pets,
- Rules on alteration of property,
- Painting restrictions,
- Instructions for parking vehicles,
- The process for requesting repairs,
- Rental due dates and late fees,
- How to remit payment, and

Any other rule or regulation that the tenant should know.

Leases can be two pages or 20 pages. While there are dozens of free leases that can be downloaded online, it is best to have a real estate attorney review or prepare the agreement for you.

7. Manage property

Property management includes:

- Selection of new tenants;
- Management of leases and moves;
- Coordinate tenant maintenance requests;

- Communicate with tenants;
- Collect the rent;
- Send notices, including eviction notices and late payments;
- Moving inspections; Y
- Disbursement of deposit fees after move-in.

There are two options when it comes to property management: hire a third party or do it yourself.

Use a third party management company

If the goal of the rental property is to generate passive income, it is probably best to hire a property management company. They take care of everything related to the management of the rent in exchange for monthly payments.

Each management company has a different structure for its fees and services, which can be a flat fee or a percentage of gross income. You will often pay 8-12% of your rents.

Interview the management company before hiring them. Ask for referrals from other clients, visit other properties they manage, and look for reviews online to make sure they deliver what they promise.

Manage the property yourself

If you decide to manage the property yourself, consider using a free online rental service like Cozy or Avail, which allows you to:

- Deposit all payments directly into your bank account. Collect deposits and rent online,
- Manage the lease (including sending electronic signatures),
- Send automatic reminders via text or email that rent is overdue or payment is late
- Automatically calculate if a fee is due for being overdue, and

One of the last active roles involved in managing a rental property is handling repairs and maintenance. As a landlord, it's best to be proactive with maintenance so you don't have to deal with emergency repairs. Before the tenant moves in, make sure the property is in good working order.

It can be helpful to provide your tenant with reminders or even supplies for routine maintenance, such as changing the air filter.

Many homeowners create a list of local service professionals, such as handymen, plumbers, electricians, and contractors. If an unexpected repair arises, the owner knows exactly who to call to resolve the problem quickly.

Before the tenant moves in, take a tour of the property. Take time-stamped photographs of each room and record the condition of the property on an inspection report. The tenant and the landlord must sign this agreement at the time of move-in and move-in.

This agreement shows the tenant your expectations about the condition of the rental upon moving out and allows them to check the initial condition if there are disparities. When moving out, use this same checklist to reevaluate the conditions and determine the portion of the deposit the tenant receives.

CHAPTER TWO

Common Rental Property Mistakes Beginners Make

Miscalculate the demand in the area

Don't buy a property in a market that doesn't support your investment just because you thought it would be a great place to invest. This is important for all types of rental properties, but it is especially important for vacation rentals.

Supply and demand

Determine the success or failure of your rental property. Make a research on supply and demand in your area. Find a real-time average vacancy rate for your property type. These will tell you if it is a viable place to invest. You can find vacancy rates in census data, and local agents and property managers can provide you with up-to-date information on vacancies.

Underestimating expenses and overestimating rents

New investors are often excited at the prospect of owning a rental property and overestimate the net rent.

It's best to err on the side of caution and run your numbers at a slightly lower than average rental rate.

If your calculations look good with this number, a market rental will be even better. Doing this leaves flexibility in your rental price in the event of changes in the market or if there is more supply than demand for your type of rental in that area.

Before buying a rental, confirm your estimated expenses. Research the annual tax rate, get a rental property insurance quote, and look at historical utility bills.

CHAPTER THREE

A Landlord's Guide to Late Payment Fees

Are you thinking of imposing a late fee payment on your tenants?

As a landlord, you depend on your tenants paying their rent consistently and on time. It's how you cover repairs and maintenance, keep cash flow, and simply put, how you keep your business afloat.

But as with anything in this business, there is no hard and fast rule about how late fees work. When should the charge take effect? Should I offer a grace period before adding the fee? And if you charge one, how much is appropriate? This guide can answer all of those questions and more.

What is a late fee?

A late payment fee is basically an additional charge that is added to the tenant's existing rent payment when he or she does not pay on time. Most landlords charge them, and as long as they are included in the lease from the beginning, it is legal to charge them if the tenant breaks the rules.

You don't have to charge a late rent fee, of course, and there are definitely trade-offs to doing so. On the positive side, late fees help encourage payments on time and compensate for late bills in case the late rent hits your finances.

The downside is that they could make paying back rent even more difficult for your tenant. If they are really in financial trouble, adding more to their debt will not help them pay it off, but may make them less likely to pay their bill.

Most states have laws on how high late rent rates can go, so check with your local housing department or a real estate attorney in your area to see what laws you must follow. Here in Texas, for example, you cannot charge more than 10% to 12% of the monthly rent, depending on the size of your property.

Generally speaking, most landlords opt for less than that, usually around 5% of the rent. On a $ 1,200 unit, that would mean a $ 60 fee. You can also go for a simple flat fee instead of calculating a percentage. Under this model, $ 50 to $ 75 is pretty standard.

In some states, you can also charge fees for each day your rent is late. Be aware that these can add up, making it even more difficult for the tenant to pay off his debts. (It could even lead to eviction).

Payment best practices for late payment

If you choose to charge late fees, there are some general rules you should follow.

1. Input your late payment fee policies in your rental agreement with your tenant

You should make the late rent charge legally binding and make sure your tenant is well aware of the policy before moving into the property. The document for the lease must clarify the actual date for late payment, and it must also indicate the actual amount of charge for late payment.

2. Have a grace period

It is common to offer tenants a grace period, usually three to five days between the due date of the rent and the time the late payment fee will be officially applied. If you choose to offer a grace period, make sure you are aware of when a tenant entered. Take time to notify them that rent is due and any default in paying rent on time attracts a late payment fee. This will often motivate them to pay before it's too late.

3. Be prepared to ignore late fees.

If a tenant's rent is regularly late, late fees are likely not to be taken seriously either. In this case, you will need to remove late fees from your security deposit when you move in. If this happens, be sure to document any unpaid late fees and include them in your itemized expense list when deducting from your security deposit.

Have a constantly late tenant?

You may be reading this guide because of a tenant who is routinely late and causing you problems. If that's the case, contact the tenant and find out more about their circumstances. There is a chance that your paychecks may not match the rental due date, making it difficult to consistently make payments on time. Here, you might consider adjusting the rental terms appropriately. (Pro tip: If you're concerned about making your mortgage payment, call your servicer and ask about adjusting your due date as well.)

You can also enable credit card payments. Sometimes tenants only need a few days to gather the cash needed for the rent. Allowing card payments allows them to finance the rent for that short period and then pay for it on their own time as they see fit.

The bottom line

Late payment fees are standard practice for most rental property investors. If you are considering charging your tenants for one, be sure to study local laws, calculate a reasonable late fee, and include a detailed policy in your lease.

If you need additional guidance, contact a real estate attorney in your area. They can tell you what local rules and practices you need to comply with.

Six things a rental property owner cannot do

As a landlord, it is important to know what actions on your part are illegal. Here is an overview.

30

Investing in a rental property and becoming a homeowner can help you generate consistent income. But as a landlord, it is important not to cross certain boundaries in the course of selecting tenants, addressing complaints, and resolving disputes, financial or otherwise.

In fact, so that you don't end up in legal trouble, it is important that you understand what a landlord cannot do when he manages a building and the tenants who live there.

1. *Enter a tenant's home without warning*

As a landlord, you have the right to enter a tenant's rental unit without prior notice if a true emergency arises, such as a fire or gas leak. Otherwise, you must notify tenants well in advance before entering their homes. Each state sets its own laws regarding proper entry notice, and the specific amount you must give must also be outlined in your lease, so be sure to follow those rules.

2. *Raising a tenant's rent without prior notice*.

You may incur additional expenses while managing a building or home, but you can't just pass those costs on to your tenants overnight. If you are increasing a tenant's rent, you should be prepared to give proper notice. Usually, this implies a 30days minimum. Again, the details should be detailed in your rental agreement.

Also, if you are renting a rent-controlled or rent-stabilized apartment, be very careful about following the rules. Rent control laws vary by city and state, but generally set a limit on how much a tenant's rent can increase when a lease is filed to renew. That limit is generally based on factors like the local cost of living and inflation.

But if a tenant moves out of a rental-controlled unit, that unit is deregulated, at which point you are free to collect market rent according to what your other tenants are paying. However, there may be exceptions, so carefully review your local city or state guidelines when dealing with rent control situations.

3. Refusing to make reasonable repairs

It is the landlord's duty to ensure that all rental units are safe and habitable, so refusing to make reasonable repairs could result in the tenant taking legal action against them, especially if the issues in question compromise the safety or health of the tenant. Tenant. For example, if there's lead paint or mold on a unit on his property and it doesn't fix the problem, you could end up being the subject of a lawsuit. So be prepared to properly maintain his property and address valid tenant concerns.

4. Withhold the tenant's security deposit

It is common to collect a security deposit at the beginning of a lease, usually a month's rent, to cover damage to a rental unit caused by a tenant. In many states, you must place that security deposit in an escrow account for the term of your tenant's lease.

While you are allowed to keep a security deposit if a tenant causes significant damage to your rental property, you cannot keep that security deposit to cover the cost of repairing normal wear and tear. And if you try to keep that money for an invalid reason, your tenant can sue you in small claims court.

That said, most states allow landlords to keep a security deposit if a tenant breaks a lease early. That way, the deposit can cover the unpaid rent.

5. Evict a tenant without going through the proper channels

You may come across a scenario where a tenant refuses to pay rent or follow the rules outlined in their lease. In that situation, he may be tempted to take action by locking the tenant out of his unit and removing his personal belongings from the premises. But if he doesn't follow the proper legal channels, you could end up with an illegal eviction on his hands, which could harm you more than your tenant.

Before attempting to drive a delinquent tenant to the curb, you must provide that tenant with a formal notice of eviction stating that the tenant must either remedy the problem in question (for example, catch up on the rent) or vacate the property for a certain date (you will need to check your local laws to see how much time you should spend).

If your tenant does not comply, your next step is to file your eviction in court, after which you will be given an eviction hearing date. If a judge rules in your favor during that hearing, you will get an eviction warrant, which your tenant must comply with. If the tenant still refuses to move out, they will need to go to the local sheriff's department or law enforcement agency to have that tenant and accompanying belongings removed from their property.

Unfortunately, the eviction process can be lengthy and expensive, but you will need to follow the rules to avoid legal backlash. Also, at some point, you may be subject to eviction moratoriums. For example, moratoriums were put in place during the coronavirus crisis to protect tenants. Violating an eviction ban could get you in serious trouble, so pay attention to applicable laws and consult an attorney before taking action.

6. Refusing to rent to a tenant based on race or other discriminatory factors

As a landlord, you have every right to screen tenants and deny someone based on bad credit or financial red flags. However, it is illegal to deny a potential tenant a lease based on the following factors:

- Race
- Skin color
- Religion
- National origin
- Gender
- Family state
- Disability

It's all part of the Fair Housing Act, which you may want to familiarize yourself with if you're new to homeownership. Not only is it illegal to refuse to rent to someone based on these factors, it is also illegal to discriminate against certain tenants by offering them lease terms that are less favorable than what you are giving to other tenants. For example, you cannot increase a tenant's rent or impose additional restrictions based on any of the factors listed above.

CHAPTER FOUR

What is property management?

Rental property management is the art where an entity is given charge for maintaining the status quo of property and appeasing tenants. Property managers, therefore, are traditionally hired by rental property owners to oversee the day-to-day operations of their real estate assets and address any questions or concerns that tenants may have. In the event the property is vacant, the property managers' job is to make sure the home is rented. As the name suggests, property management takes care of all aspects of a rental home, from marketing vacant space and signing leases to collecting rent and requesting repairs. Few strategies, for that matter, are more beneficial to a rental portfolio than hiring an outside property manager, which raises a simple question: How do property management companies work?

How to get an experienced property manager for a rental property

First, you need to find potential property managers; there are a few sources for these:

Referrals: If you know someone else who owns a professionally managed rental property, ask for a referral. You can also try with your property manager and even friends who rent and have good relationships with the managers responsible for their properties.

Yelp - Many local property management companies are listed on Yelp, so a quick search there should return some results, with the added benefit of being able to see what others have said about them.

Google - Large property management companies (as well as some smaller ones) have websites, so a simple Google search for "property management <your area>" should generate some prospects.

Once you have located at least a few prospects, you need to examine them and choose the one that is right for you. Some things to look for:

Experience - Not just general experience as a property manager, but experience specific to your property type and market. A manager who primarily manages downtown luxury apartments may not be the right manager for a low-level duplex in a poorer area.

References - Be sure to ask for a couple of references and follow up on them. Ask more direct questions about how the property manager works with them.

Personality - Your PM is someone you will trust with a very valuable asset and a significant amount of money. This means that you will have to deal with them regularly, so be sure to hire someone you can get along with.

Tasks Performed by Rental Property Manager You Should Know About

What do property managers do?

• Advertising for tenants

• Tenant detection

• Inspections and maintenance

• Rent collection

• Evictions or work with judges

•   Reports

• Accepts trouble tickets from tenants and contractors

• Accept trouble tickets from owners

Here are some important questions to ask a rental property manager in an interview

Fictitious warning: don't be an idiot asking these questions. Let him guide a conversation instead of playing the fool. You need a good property manager more than a good property manager needs you ... does that make sense?!?

Remember to create a level of connection with this person. Can they have an intelligent conversation that will give you the answer from the textbook?

- How long have you rendered the services of a rental property manager?
- What kind of properties do you manage?
- What type of insurance do you have? What if someone sues me?
- How many units do you currently manage?
- How many assistant property managers and property managers does your company have?
- What associations do you belong to?
- How many vacancies do you have right now?
- Average Time to fill a vacancy Leasing structure?
- Have a sample lease? Do you have an initial 1 or 2-year lease?
- What is your late rental policy?
- Do you keep the late fees or the landlord?

- Do you conduct regular property inspections? How often?
- What percentage of tenants are evicting?
- What is an eviction and process charge?
- What are the management fees?
- Any other fees? (Cancellation, eviction, lease renewal ($ 200-500, or nothing), marketing, account setup)
- How much do you charge to find a new tenant and lease?
- Do you charge a fee when my units are unoccupied?
- If I actually decide to sell my property, is it mandatory I list it with you?
- How do you market your properties?
- What is your repair process?
- How do you handle communication with me? Through a portal? Phone calls?
- How do you select prospects?
- When will I receive my monthly net income?
- Do you make direct deposits? Can tenants pay rent electronically?
- Referrals if available to speak

Property management tips for the first time buyers

- It's a job. Never forget that. If you manage a property yourself, you are buying a job.
- Ask yourself what the objective of your investment is. Seriously.
- If your goal is to be a property manager or eventually create a property management company, then by all means, self-manage your first rental. It is important to acquire that experience.
- If your goal is pretty much anything else, my advice is not to manage it at all. In your business analysis, always include an expense of 8-12% (depending on your area) of the gross rent for property management. If an offer still works with that expense included, great. When you buy the place, delegate the management to a professional manager.

Why?

Over time, you will want to have more and more rentals, right? With each additional unit you buy, you will need to spend more time managing it. That takes away the time you could spend searching for and financing more deals. And even if you're happy with the size of your wallet, do you want the 3 a.m. phone calls about clogged toilets?

How to manage rental property the right way.

Managing property the right way simply indicates sincerity, work, and communication. At the end of the day, you need to set the right expectations by going the extra mile and making sure you have clear lines of communication open. One of the ways you can find yourself in trouble is if you set the wrong expectations and fail to communicate.

For example, when it comes to short-term rentals, if you describe a feature that isn't available in a property, it's not the end of the world. But, if you fail to communicate that error to the guest and allow the problem to escalate, you could have a major issue on your hands that is likely to result in a complaint. Communication here is the key. Each dispute can be resolved with the appropriate amount of communication and by determining exactly what issue needs to be resolved.

1. *Know your home*

When you first buy a new property, your first step should be to really get to know the home and all of the systems that comprise it. Each of the systems in your home has a specific service interval and lifespan. The last thing you want to happen when you rent your home is for one of these systems to fail, caused by a lack of maintenance or preventative care.

2. *Create a financial plan*

Understand a lot that your home is likely to generate income, which depends on three key factors.

The specific location within the destination

The luxury level of the home.

Its size and amenities

Professional vacation rental management companies use data to accurately predict a home's income. Without access to that data, you will have to do your due diligence and track websites and research fees. However, the advertised rates are not always a prediction of the income you can expect to receive and you will be far removed from the knowledge related to occupancy rates.

3. *Endeavor to require the services of an experienced real estate agent*

A real estate agent's knowledge of the vacation rental business is often mixed. Some have great first-hand insight into the industry. Others know little or nothing about it. And, while they may be able to offer property management advice regardless of your experience, it is important that you work with agents who understand the business, especially in the early stages of finding, buying, and managing homes that are intended to be used as vacation rentals.

4. *Browse multiple property managers*

Before hiring a property manager, especially one who manages vacation rentals, be sure to interview several companies. Do they have a local presence? What kind of reputation do they have? Do they rank high in search engines like Google for searches relevant to your particular area?

Maximizing Your Home Generated Income

Taking proper care of your home and guarantying an overwhelming experience whenever you come back

Provide transparent and honest communications

5. *Provide easy-to-use instructions.*

When guests go on vacation and rent a home, they don't want to waste all their time figuring out how to use that home. Make it simple for them. How are A / V systems used? What about television, cable, or Apple TV? How about some music system or the laundry room? The big property management companies will really review and detail all of this so you don't have to do it yourself. But, if you do it on your own, be serious with it.

6. Ensure adequate inventory levels

One of the main reasons that guests rent houses and travel in groups is so they can cook and eat together. Some of the best memories that are created relate to the dining and dining experience of the guests. So don't get in the way of lacking kitchen essentials. Properly store kitchen and other household essentials to make sure nothing is missing. If you are unsure, find a great property management company to help you identify what is missing.

7. be strategic about personal use

Peak periods for vacation rentals, which generally revolve around the summer or winter seasons, also known as peak seasons, and get 2-3 times the income, sometimes even more. If you are staying at home, be strategic when you go. Do not take up too much of the calendar during peak hours, as you risk reducing the revenue that could be generated. Try to stick to the off-season as much as possible.

8. Think of your home as a hospitality business.

If you are running your home like a rental, treat it like a hospitality business. The care and attention that most elegant hotels put into their facilities and rooms is second to none. While a property management company can help you with this, if you go it alone, you need a genuine desire to please your guests. Treat them like friends or family. If it feels more like a nuisance to you, then you shouldn't manage guests because your reviews will ultimately reflect the negative experience received.

CHAPTER FIVE

How rental properties make money

Rental properties, foundations, introduction, retirement

How rental properties make money

It's no secret that a well-located and reasonably priced real estate investment can effectively generate more income than the cost of the money used to finance it.

Many of those who have held onto single-family homes in good areas for 10 years or more have accumulated substantial amounts of capital and many savings.

They include:

- Cash flow
- Amortization
- Appreciation
- Fiscal benefits

1. *Cash flow*

The most recommended method a rental property can make a reasonable income is through cash flow. Simply put, this is the difference between the rent charged and all operating expenses. Go!

For example, let's say you buy a house for $ 200,000 and rent it for $ 1,500 per month. If you get a great interest rate and make a healthy down payment, your "PITI" (principal, interest, taxes, and insurance) would be about $ 985 per month. This leaves you a difference of $ 515 between the rent you charge and the monthly PITI payment.

Is it really that simple? Of course, no! To comprehend the amount of money you will actually be making here, we need to discuss the term Net operating income.

What is net operating income?

Net operating income (NOI) is the rent you charge, less all operating expenses. The most common operating expenses are:

Vacant (when your property is empty)

Repairs (when your property needs repairs)

Management fees (to find/evict tenants and pay attention to detail)

Late payment (when tenants pay late or stop paying altogether)

To do the calculation for [N.O.I], you can times the monthly rent by 12 ($ 1,000 x 12) = $ 12,000; this is often called to as scheduled gross rent.

Now let's look at the expenses.

Vacancy allowance

A vacancy is a time between tenants. When a tenant moves out, the property must be "surrendered" to be ready to rent. You will need to acknowledge that no rent will be charged during this period and as such, you should realistically budget for the lost rent. To be conservative, I like to assume that my property will remain vacant for a full month out of the year.

So let's deduct a month's rent of $ 1,500 from our previous scheduled gross rent.

$ 18,000 - $ 1,500 = $ 16,500

Repair

These are the daily maintenance items such as faucets, appliances, doors, locks, light fixtures, HVAC repair, etc. This amount may vary based on the size and age of the property but on average a decent benchmark. For a new home in good condition, it is approximately $ 2,000 per year.

Let's deduct another $ 2,000 from our scheduled gross rent.

$ 18,000 - $ 1,500 - $ 2,000 = $ 14,500

Management fees

Unlike vacancies and repairs, this is a discretionary expense. However, you do not need to hire a property manager; someone will have to manage all the properties you own (even if it is YOU), so it is wise to recognize this very real cost.

I like to manage my own properties so I will not pay this money to a third-party property management company, but I am very experienced and pay the price on my time.

You must decide for yourself whether you want to go it alone or hire a manager. Many property management companies will charge approximately 10% of the gross rent ($ 18,000 x 10%) = $ 1,800.

Let's deduct another $ 1,800 from the GSR.

$ 18,000 - $ 1,500 - $ 2,000 - $ 1,800 = $ 12,700

Delinquency

This cost is a bit more difficult to predict compared to vacancies and repairs. Assuming you are buying a good home in a good part of town and your tenants are being properly screened, this shouldn't be a problem.

Let's cut another $ 360 from our gross rent for the year.

As you can see above, your net operating income is your scheduled gross rent subtracted from all operating expenses (and note that the mortgage is not part of this calculation).

Mortgage (PITI)

The payment of Principal, Interest, Taxes, and Insurance (or "PITI" for short) will be your largest expense and will include the total amount of Principle, Interest, Taxes, and Insurance for the year.

Now let's look at the numbers...

After these expenses, you will have a profit of $ 520 for the year, which is not a lot of money.

However, it is important to recognize that if you had a management company that did all the basic work, it would be passive income that would require virtually no time or work on your part.

Also, if rental prices should increase over time, your gross rents will rise while principal and interest payments remain the way it was.

Ending the year with $ 2,320 isn't a bad deal (assuming you didn't spend a large amount of your time managing the property), but what else do you get for your investment?

2 Amortization (Initial Payment)

With each monthly payment made on your loan, a portion of that payment goes toward paying the principal amount owed on the property.

The key point to remember here is that you will pay your mortgage with someone else's money (the rent you receive from your tenant).

If you have ever looked at how a 30-year fixed mortgage is calculated, you will see that with each passing year, you pay progressively more principle than the previous year. This means that you are building equity (the difference between the value of the property and the principal balance of the loan) each year with someone else's money.

The details of how mortgages are amortized is another matter; For now, all you need to remember is that each time you enter a rent payment, a progressively larger portion of your Principal and Interest payment goes towards your mortgage payment, which effectively accumulates your equity with your tenant's money.

As you can see in Chart 1 below, you'd be paying $ 3,166.56 upfront in Year 1, effectively increasing your net worth (all of your assets minus your liabilities) by just over $ 3,000.

Again, the money is not much as expected, I get it!

Always have in mind that, buying and holding real estate is a longer-term strategy. Let's look at things around the fifth year.

As you can see above, at the end of the fifth year you have added an additional $ 17K to your net worth, and you have done so with your tenant's rent.

3. Appreciation

The average home appreciation rate is highly dependent on local factors, as well as some booms and busts in the US economy.

To avoid getting bogged down in complicated financial data, I like to be conservative in assuming that a good home in a good area will appreciate an average of 1% per year.

4. Fiscal benefits

Real estate gives some of the best tax advantages to the asset classes. Rental properties can be depreciated each year to offset any cash flow, and all maintenance and expenses can be deducted from earnings received.

Remember the $ 5,700 in mortgage interest you paid in the first year? Everything is tax-deductible. So any cash flow you made at the end of the first year, whether it's $

500 + (managed by a professional company) or $ 2,000 + (if you manage it yourself) would be offset by the mortgage interest you paid. You also have the option of deducting that mortgage interest from any personal income you earned that year.

Why is the value of a rental property appreciating?

Home appreciation is not always guaranteed, so it helps to start with an understanding of why appreciation occurs in the first place.

Fixed supply

There is a fixed supply of land to build houses in the United States. The increasing population gradually increases demand, and with a fixed supply of land, this will naturally drive up the price.

Population growth

The United States has experienced a steady increase in population over time. More people means that more roofs are needed to house them.

According to the Wake County Demographics Study, Raleigh is growing at a rate of 14% annually. This increase in population increases the demand for housing which increases the price. Make out time for rates in your territory. Many counties, like Wake County, NC, will post demographic data that they share with the public.

CHAPTER SIX

Conclusion

Rental property management companies, specifically the good ones, are worth their weight in gold. It is entirely possible for a really good rental property manager to save/earn investors more money than their initial fees. Also, the cost of property management is likely to be an investment in disguise than viewing as an expense. There is no reason to believe that the use of rental property management companies cannot elevate even a new investor's career to the next level.